O9-AID-827

Where Is the Great Barrier Reef?

by Nico Medina

illustrated by John Hinderliter

Grosset & Dunlap
An Imprint of Penguin Random House

For David Lloyd, aka Captain Slick,
Bassmaster—NM

For Ruby and Rose, who love animals,
even underwater ones—JH

GROSSET & DUNLAP
Penguin Young Readers Group
An Imprint of Penguin Random House LLC

Text copyright © 2016 by Nico Medina. Illustrations copyright © 2016 by Penguin Random House LLC. All rights reserved. Published by Grosset & Dunlap, an imprint of Penguin Random House LLC, 345 Hudson Street, New York, New York 10014. Who HQ™ and all related logos are trademarks owned by Penguin Random House LLC. GROSSET & DUNLAP is a trademark of Penguin Random House LLC. Printed in the USA.

Library of Congress Cataloging-in-Publication Data is available.

ISBN 9780448486994 (paperback)   10 9 8 7 6 5 4 3 2 1
ISBN 9780399542398 (library binding)   10 9 8 7 6 5 4 3 2 1

Contents

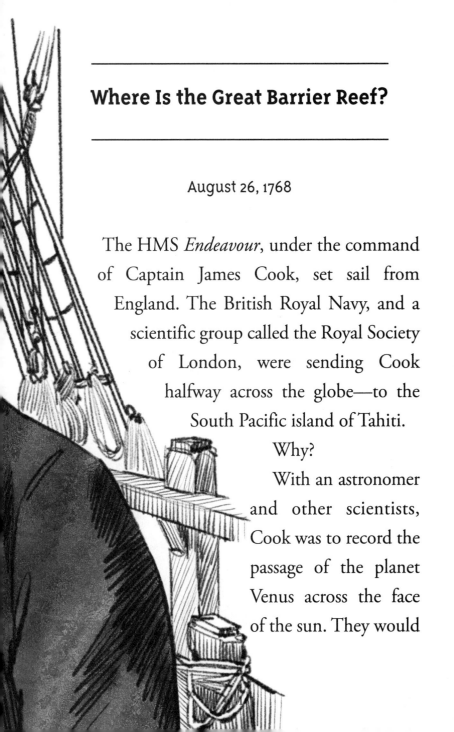

Where Is the Great Barrier Reef?

August 26, 1768

The HMS *Endeavour*, under the command of Captain James Cook, set sail from England. The British Royal Navy, and a scientific group called the Royal Society of London, were sending Cook halfway across the globe—to the South Pacific island of Tahiti.

Why?

With an astronomer and other scientists, Cook was to record the passage of the planet Venus across the face of the sun. They would

1

compare their measurements to measurements other astronomers were taking around the world. This would help them figure out the distance between the earth and the sun.

Months later, in June 1769, the work in Tahiti was done. But Captain Cook was not going home. Not yet. He had been given a sealed letter before he left England. Now he could open it. The letter contained a set of orders for a second mission—a secret mission.

Cook was to sail from Tahiti to a place known only as *Terra Australis Incognita*. This is Latin for "Unknown South Land." Today, we call it Australia.

Forty-year-old Captain Cook was a very experienced sailor and explorer. The British Royal Navy wanted him to explore Australia's east coast. No European had ever seen this land.

On April 19, 1770, the *Endeavour* reached this part of Australia. Cook later named it New South Wales and claimed it for England.

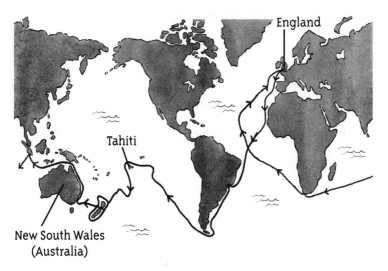

Cook's Voyage

The States of Australia

At the time of Cook's voyage, Australia had not yet been settled by Europeans. It was called either Terra Australis Incognita or New Holland—named by the Dutch sailors from Holland who had explored its western shores.

In the 1780s, people from England began to move to Australia. In 1788, a border between New South Wales in the east and New Holland in the west was established. In 1829, England claimed all of Australia.

The English established colonies—much like the thirteen original colonies of the United States. In 1901, Australia became its own country with six states, plus federal territories and a capital district.

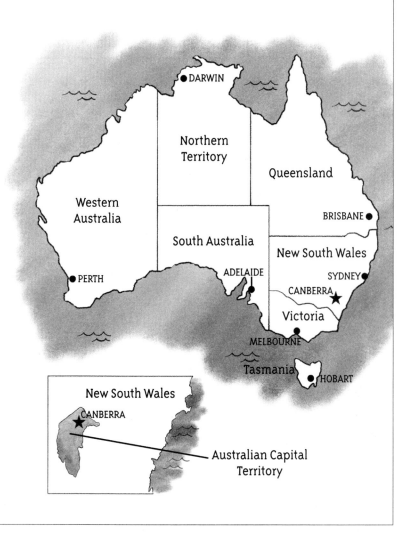

States of Australia and Their Capitals

Captain Cook continued north along the coast. He didn't know he was about to make another great discovery—a dangerous discovery.

Late on June 11, under a bright moon, the *Endeavour* crashed into something rock solid! The ship became stuck! Cook and his crew were twelve miles from shore. They tried to move the ship back into deep water by lightening the ship's load. They threw as much as fifty tons of cannons, coal, and cargo overboard. They waited until morning, hoping that the high tide would lift the ship. But it stayed stuck.

A leak sprung. Water poured into the ship. For the next twelve hours, the men scrambled to save their ship. They took turns at the pumps, trying to push seawater out as fast as it poured in. One sailor filled a canvas sail with wool and sheep's dung and used it to help plug the leak.

Around ten o'clock that night, high tide arrived again. The crew was able to guide the *Endeavour* off its rocky ledge and back into deep water. They were saved!

This "rocky ledge," however, was not actually rock at all. It was a coral reef. Coral is made up of millions of tiny animals called polyps (PAWL-lups). This coral reef was one of three thousand reefs that make up the Great Barrier Reef.

For more than six weeks, Captain Cook and his crew repaired the *Endeavour* onshore. More than two months after the crash, Cook was finally able to steer the ship through the Reef and out into the open ocean.

Captain Cook's "discovery" of the Great Barrier Reef was only the beginning. Ever since, this miracle of nature has captured the imagination of explorers, scientists, and tourists alike. Today, more than a million people visit the Great Barrier Reef each year. And we've only just begun to understand it.

CHAPTER 1
Islands from Hilltops

The Great Barrier Reef is enormous. It is the largest living structure on earth.

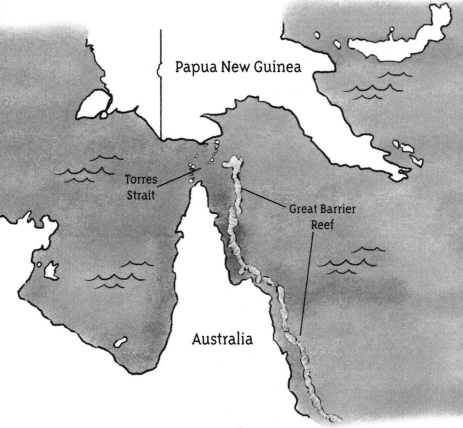

Papua New Guinea

Torres Strait

Great Barrier Reef

Australia

It is *so* big, it can be seen from outer space! From high above the earth, it looks almost like a line of turquoise-colored toothpaste between the green of Australia and the deep blue of the Pacific Ocean. Closer up, the colors begin to change.

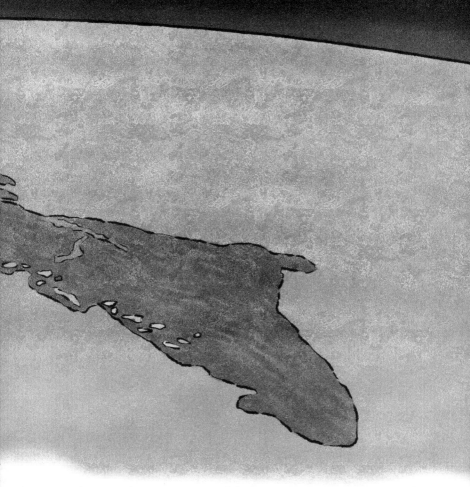

The reefs appear reddish brown just beneath the water's surface. White, sandy islands dot the seascape. Lush green islands covered in rain forests rise up from the sea. Shallow water surrounding the islands shines bright aquamarine.

Below the surface, the Great Barrier Reef presents visitors with an eye-popping spectacle. Snorkelers and scuba divers can swim amid creatures of every color. Orange-and-white-striped lionfish. Purple crabs. Schools of pink

anthia fish. Blue-and-black surgeonfish wriggling their bright-yellow tails to glide through the water. There are walls of coral in reds and pinks, giant clams with gaping multicolored mouths, and sea anemones with green tentacles.

The Great Barrier Reef is not one giant coral reef. It is a system of three thousand individual reefs. More than 1,400 miles long, it is the largest coral-reef system in the world. It is longer than the distance between Seattle and San Diego! About 10 percent of the world's coral reefs are contained in the Great Barrier Reef.

Coral Reefs Around the World

From the Caribbean Sea to the Indian Ocean, wherever the water is warm, clear, and shallow, and the sun shines bright, coral reefs exist. The largest area of coral reefs is in the waters surrounding Indonesia, the Philippines, and Southeast Asia. The world's second-longest coral reef lies between northeast Africa and the Arabian Peninsula, in the Red Sea. Florida Reef, the only coral reef in the continental United States, stretches 220 miles along the Florida Keys. It is protected as an underwater state park, the first of its kind in the United States.

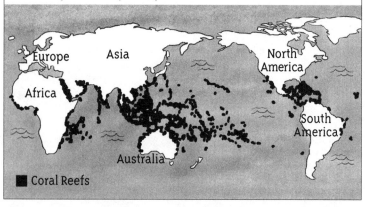

Coral Reefs

The Great Barrier Reef gets its name because it forms a sort of *barrier*, blocking the open ocean from the shore. It protects the mainland from storms and powerful ocean waves.

There are more than six hundred islands in the Great Barrier Reef. If you include the islands in the Torres Strait (the body of water between Australia and Papua New Guinea), it's closer to one thousand!

A few thousand years ago, some of these islands weren't islands at all. They were actually limestone hills on the mainland!

How is this possible?

It's because about a hundred thousand years ago, the world grew colder. Much of the water on the earth's surface became ice. Glaciers and ice caps grew larger. As more water in the oceans froze, the sea level dropped by more than four hundred feet. In Australia, coral reefs that had been underwater were now above the surface.

The Ice Age

When people think of the Ice Age, they probably think of animals like the woolly mammoth or the saber-toothed tiger. But the planet has actually been through many different "ice ages."

The oldest ice age we know began more than two billion years ago. During this time, the entire planet was frozen over, and the earth was like one giant snowball. Three more major ice ages would come and go before dinosaurs appeared.

Within each major ice age, there are both warm and cool periods. Our most recent ice age began about 2.5 million years ago and is still going on. The cool period most people think of as the "Ice Age"—the Ice Age with cavemen and mammoths—began about a hundred thousand years ago and ended twelve thousand years ago.

Once the coral reefs were above water, they began to die and became hard. After many years, sun, wind, and rain turned these dead reefs into limestone hills. Mud and sediment washed up and over them. Eventually, plants and trees began to grow. Animals moved in. What once was a coral reef was now an all-new grassy landscape.

Then, about eighteen thousand years ago, the earth's climate started to heat back up. Ice melted into the oceans. For the next twelve thousand years, the sea level rose about half an inch every year.

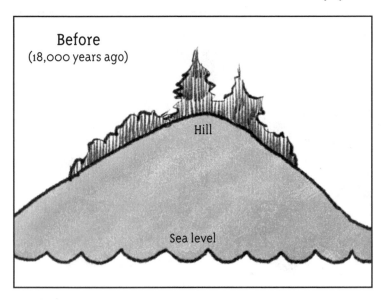

Before
(18,000 years ago)

Hill

Sea level

Over time, the ocean swallowed up the land and covered up most of the limestone hills.

Today, the tops of those old limestone hills are surrounded by water. They are among the islands we see in the Great Barrier Reef today.

Many of these islands are surrounded by coral reefs. Today, on some islands there are popular tourist destinations. On others there are research centers, where people learn more about the Great Barrier Reef. But most of the islands remain pure wilderness, untouched by humans.

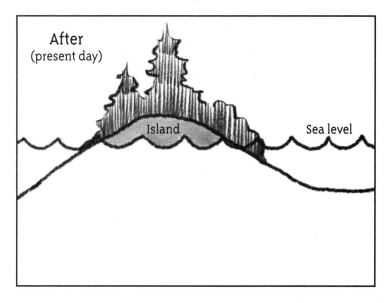

After
(present day)

Island

Sea level

Raine Island

Raine Island—less than half the size of Disneyland in California—is an island in the Great Barrier Reef.

In the late 1800s, the British mined Raine Island for rock. They built a lighthouse on the island out of this rock and wood from a shipwreck. The Raine Island beacon is still there.

Raine Island is a wildlife sanctuary. People can't go there anymore. It is a nesting ground for many species—or types—of birds. Raine Island is also one of the largest and most important nesting grounds in the world for green sea turtles. More than forty thousand sea turtles lay their eggs on Raine Island in a typical nesting season!

CHAPTER 2
The First Reef People

The first people to live around the Great Barrier Reef were the Torres Strait Islanders and the Aboriginal Australians, or Aborigines (ab-or-IDGE-i-neez).

Torres Strait Islander

Aborigines playing didgeridoos

About fifty thousand years ago, these people came to Australia from Southeast Asia. When sea levels dropped, more land became exposed, and the Aborigines moved out to the water's edge. Then, when the water rose again, some settled on the new islands, and others moved to the mainland.

The Continental Shelf

The edge of a continent that extends into the ocean and lies underwater is called the *continental shelf*. The width and depth of the continental shelf is different from place to place but is usually around forty miles wide and two hundred feet deep.

When sea levels dropped, the east Australian continental shelf became land. It was hilly and covered in trees. Tribes of native peoples lived there. Wallabies and koala bears lived there, too. But when the ocean rose back up, the continental shelf went back underwater.

Today, the east Australian continental slope is home to the Great Barrier Reef.

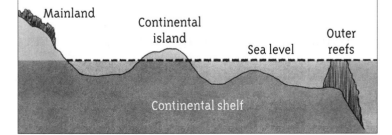

There are more than seventy Aboriginal and Torres Strait Islander tribes still living around the Great Barrier Reef today. But thousands of years ago, there were as many as six hundred tribes! Many tribes spoke their own language. But none of them had a written language. Instead, they passed on their beliefs through fables, cave paintings, and songs. They continue to do this today.

Cave painting

Some of their stories are nearly thirteen thousand years old. They are among the first stories ever told on the planet. One is about a great flood—when the sea rose and drowned the coastal plain.

While each tribe had its own language, many people spoke more than just their native tongue. That's because different Aboriginal tribes often came into contact with one another. They traded goods and grew to know one another. They also held gatherings for special occasions, like sea-turtle hunts.

The ancient people of the Great Barrier Reef believed they belonged to the land and the sea. Before modern times, they depended on both for their survival.

The land provided fruit and seeds, and stones used to make tools. Grasses and tree bark soaked in water could be made into fishing lines, ropes, and nets.

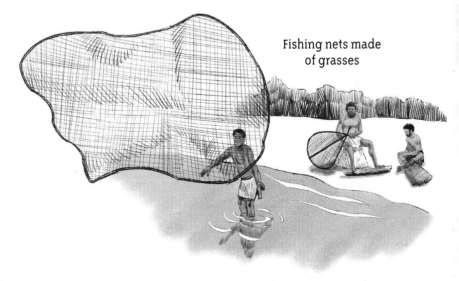

Fishing nets made of grasses

The sea provided food—fish, oysters, stingrays, sea turtles. Parts of these animals could be made into tools. Sharkskin was used as sandpaper. Spines from stingrays were made into spear tips. Shells and bones could be turned into fishhooks.

The Aborigines were clever hunters. To catch big sea creatures like manta rays or sea turtles, ancient islanders sometimes used a fish called a *remora*. Also called a suckerfish, the remora has a sucker-like organ on the top of its head. It uses

Manta ray with remoras

this sucker to attach itself to a larger animal. The remora survives by eating its host's leftover food—and even its poop! Aborigines would attach a fishing line to the back fin of a remora. Next, the suckerfish was dropped into the water, where it would swim off to find a ray or turtle. Once the remora had latched on, the fisherman would slowly reel in a big meal!

Boomerangs

Aborigines came up with clever ways to hunt land animals, too.

The *boomerang* is a light, curved tool, often carved out of wood. When thrown, it can become a weapon to wound prey.

Boomerangs come in many shapes and sizes. They are broken into two main groups: returning and non-returning.

Returning boomerangs come back to the thrower after spinning through the air. Aborigines may have hunted flocks of birds with a returning boomerang. The hunter would throw the boomerang so it went past the flock. Then the boomerang would turn and go back toward the flock. This would frighten the birds. They'd fly away from the boomerang, which was "chasing" them and head straight back to the thrower! Hunters waiting with nets then would pounce on the birds, capturing them.

Non-returning boomerangs were thrown from great distances at larger animals. A boomerang thrown at high speed was said to be able to knock out a kangaroo's legs, or break an emu's neck.

The Aborigines depended on the Reef for survival. So, too, the Great Barrier Reef depends on many things for its own survival. Everything plays a part, from the sun's rays to coral-eating fish—even creatures so small, they are invisible to the naked eye.

CHAPTER 3
Coral

The building block of a reef is a tiny animal called a coral polyp. A polyp is made of a mouth lined with tentacles up top, a stomach in the middle, and a base that holds it in place. Polyps have naturally clear bodies, with no color. Most coral polyps are around a quarter inch wide, but some can grow up to a foot in length!

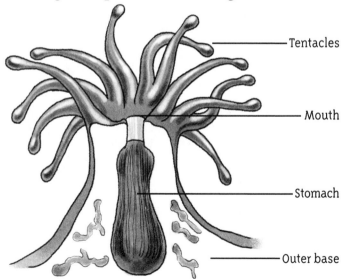

Tentacles

Mouth

Stomach

Outer base

There are six hundred known species of coral in the Great Barrier Reef. More are still being discovered. There are two kinds of coral: hard coral and soft coral. When most people think of coral, they are thinking of hard coral. Hard coral is the type that builds reefs.

The polyps of a hard coral have six tentacles—or multiples of six, like twelve or eighteen. These polyps have a hard outer skeleton made of limestone. Brain, staghorn, and mushroom corals are species of hard coral. Many coral polyps are nocturnal, meaning they emerge from their coral skeletons only at night. After sundown, the polyps let their tentacles out. They reach out into the water to feed.

Brain coral

Staghorn coral

Mushroom coral

Polyps eat zooplankton—floating animals so small, they can only be seen with a microscope. Polyps can even eat small fish. Stinging cells on a polyp's tentacles stun their prey. Next, the tentacles pull the polyp's meal into its mouth.

Polyps can feed during the day, too, when their tentacles are hidden inside their coral skeletons—and they don't even have to work to get it.

Microscopic algae live inside coral polyps. In just one square inch of coral, there can be millions of them!

The micro-algae use sunlight to produce the food and energy they need.

However, the algae also produce materials they *don't* need—like proteins, sugars, and oxygen. These materials become food for the polyps. As much as 98 percent of a polyp's food comes from the algae.

Because the micro-algae inside the coral polyps need sunlight, coral reefs require clear, shallow water to survive. The shallower and clearer the water is, the more sunlight will shine through.

This arrangement works out well for both. Polyps give the algae a place to live and grow. In return, the polyps receive food. This is known as a *symbiotic* (sim-bee-AH-tick) relationship.

In a way, it's as if the polyps are "farming" the algae. They "plant" the algae within their bodies. At "harvest time," the algae give the polyp the food it needs to grow.

Algae are also what give corals their many beautiful colors!

As a coral polyp eats and grows, it produces waste of its own. One of the waste products, limestone, adds to the polyp's skeleton. This is how coral grows. Some species of coral only grow a quarter inch every year. Branching corals, which grow like tree branches, can grow as much as eight inches!

So that is how coral grows—by catching and eating prey at night, and by using algae to make food during the day. But how do corals *reproduce*? This is done through a process known as *spawning*.

Spawning occurs on just one night each year. Most corals in the Great Barrier Reef spawn on the same night. When the moonlight, the saltiness of the water, and the tide are all just right, the polyps release eggs—*trillions* of them!—into the water. It looks a lot like an upside-down underwater snowstorm!

The eggs are fertilized. Then they divide into trillions of tiny, floating larvae. If a larva is not eaten, it settles on the seafloor and attaches itself to a hard surface—a rock, or a piece of hard coral. Now the larva develops into a polyp.

Next, the polyp begins to create exact copies of itself, and divide. Eventually, these polyps form a coral colony. Hundreds or thousands of years later, a new coral reef is born!

Soft Coral

Soft corals are also made of coral polyps and can live on coral reefs, just like hard corals. However, soft corals do not build coral reefs. This is because they can't grow a hard limestone skeleton. Soft corals resemble plants and trees. They bend and sway with the ocean currents. Candelabra, fan, and toadstool corals are species of soft coral.

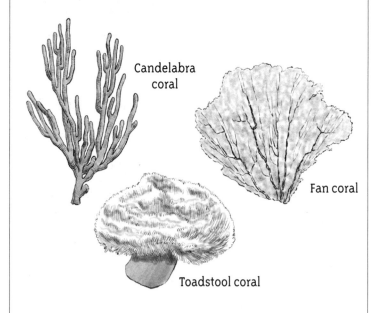

Candelabra coral

Fan coral

Toadstool coral

Reef-building hard corals need micro-algae to live. However, other types of algae can damage a coral reef. Larger *macro*-algae can grow on top of reefs. These green algae take all the sunlight for themselves. The coral underneath is able to survive only because of helpful fish such as the bumphead parrotfish.

The bumphead parrotfish is a very strange-looking fish. It gets its name from its beak-like mouth and huge forehead. It can be more than four feet long and weigh a hundred pounds. And boy, do bumpheads love algae!

Often swimming in large groups, bumpheads bite off chunks of algae-covered rock and coral with their strong jaws. After the coral is crushed

and digested, it is pooped out as sand! Over time, this "parrotfish potty" builds up to form sandy islands and beaches.

Parrotfish aren't the only animals that eat the green algae. Other species of fish—like rabbitfish, damselfish, and surgeonfish—eat algae. So do sea turtles.

Butterfly fish like algae, but they also eat the coral polyps themselves! Their long snouts root them out from their coral skeletons.

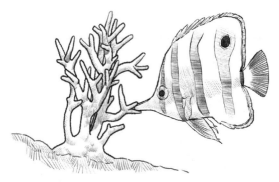

Coral reefs provide food and shelter to more than just parrotfish and other algae-eaters. They grow to form huge underwater "cities" for thousands of creatures great and small.

CHAPTER 4
Creatures of the Reef

From the tiniest algae to the largest whales, thousands of species of animals live in the Great Barrier Reef. Each serves a purpose in the community.

More than 1,700 species of fish live in the Great Barrier Reef. The Queensland grouper is one of the largest, weighing more than a thousand pounds! The grouper's mouth is so huge, it can swallow sharks and rays whole! But there is one tiny fish that the grouper lets into its mouth and does not eat.

The tiny bluestreak cleaner wrasse swims in and out of the grouper's mouth, eating dead skin and parasites. Every now and then, it vibrates its fins against the inside of the grouper's mouth.

It's reminding the grouper not to swallow it!

Grouper with wrasse

Other large animals like manta rays and sea turtles—even fearsome moray eels—also use the wrasse's "cleaning service." The wrasse actually "dances" in the water to call attention to itself, and to bring animals to its cleaning station.

Moray eel

Like the relationship between coral polyps and their micro-algae, the cleaner wrasse and its "clients" each get something they need. These relationships exist all over the Great Barrier Reef.

For example, goby fish and pistol shrimp live together in small burrows in the sand. Gobies can see very well, but the shrimp are almost blind. When outside the burrow, a shrimp uses its long antennae to stay in contact with the goby. If the goby sees danger coming, it flaps its tail and swims into the burrow, and the shrimp follows it. In return, the shrimp digs the burrow and keeps the goby's home clean. With the ever-shifting sands, it is a big job.

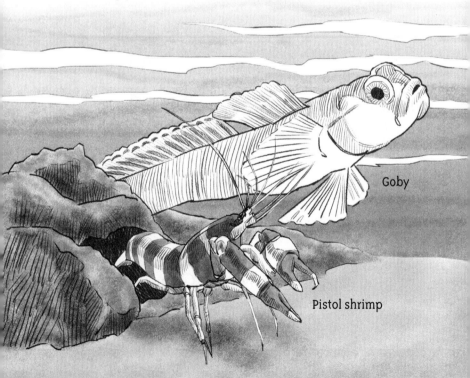

Goby

Pistol shrimp

Clownfish and sea anemones also have a symbiotic relationship. The sea anemone is a relative of the coral polyp. It has poisonous tentacles, which it uses to attack and eat fish. But the clownfish is immune to the anemone's sting. This means the sting does not affect it.

The clownfish makes the sea anemone its home. It is protected from other fish that might get stung by the anemone. In return, the clownfish eats the anemone's old, dead tentacles and keeps the area clean. (The sea anemone even feeds on clownfish poop!) The clownfish also chases away fish that want to eat the anemone.

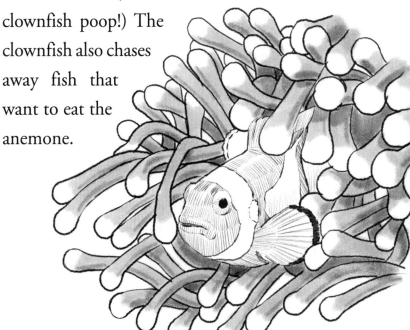

The coral reef itself provides food and shelter for many animals. Crabs, octopuses, and eels live in its nooks and crannies.

Octopus

During the day, groups of whitetips rest in caves and on the sandy ocean floor. But at night they hunt. Even in the dark, they can find their prey by using their keen sense of smell.

Whitetip reef sharks

Parrotfish have a trick for escaping the sharks. They cover up their smell by belching out a bubble of mucus. They surround themselves within this spit bubble. Then they go to sleep for the night.

Does this always work? No.

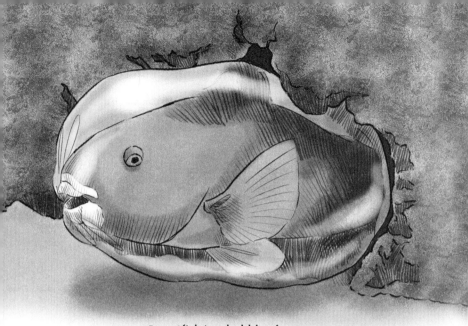

Parrotfish in a bubble of mucus

Besides having a superb sense of smell, sharks can also detect tiny movements in the water. The slender whitetip sharks are also very flexible. When they find their prey, they can wriggle into small cracks in the reef. The fish don't stand a chance.

It's not just sharks that fish have to watch out for.

The cone snail is a small but deadly fish-eater. Using its sense of smell, it sneaks up on little fish as they sleep. When it gets close enough, the snail releases a chemical, drugging the fish so it can't move. Next, the fish is swallowed alive, and a barb inside the snail kills the fish with a shot of poison. Some cone snails shoot a harpoon-like spear at their prey, then pull the fish into their mouth.

Cone snail

There are more than six hundred species of cone snails in the world. About 120 live on and around the Great Barrier Reef. One hundred different types of poison exist in *each* species of cone snail. Some of these toxins can kill a person. But they can also help people. Scientists around the world are studying cone snails. Their toxins are used to treat diseases and make medicines.

The Great Barrier
Reef is also home to ocean giants.

The whale shark is the largest fish in the
world. It grows to more than forty feet long
and weighs as much as three full-grown African
elephants. Despite its size, the whale shark is a
gentle giant. Although its mouth contains more
than three hundred rows of teeth, it doesn't eat

most sea creatures. That's because the whale shark
is a filter feeder. It feeds on krill, plankton, algae,
and tiny fish by opening its enormous mouth and
pumping water through its gills. Filters on the
inside of the gills catch its food.

Besides whale sharks, actual whales are also found around the Great Barrier Reef. From May to September, humpback whales leave the icy waters of Antarctica to visit the area. They come to the Great Barrier Reef to give birth. They raise their calves in the Reef's warm waters.

Other species of whales that live around the Reef include sperm, killer, and false killer whales. Dolphins live here, too, like the Australian snubfin, bottlenose, and spotted dolphins.

Bottlenose
dolphins

Many species of reptiles live around the Great Barrier Reef—including fourteen species of sea snakes. A sea snake looks a lot like a snake you would find on land, except its tail is shaped like a paddle. This helps it swim better. It can swim underwater for up to two hours without coming up for air. How is it able to do this? It has a large, powerful lung. Its single lung is almost as long as its entire body! Sea snakes are extremely poisonous, but they rarely bite people.

Black banded
sea krait

In addition to sea snakes, six species of sea turtles are found on the Great Barrier Reef. The olive ridley turtle is the smallest, weighing around one hundred pounds. Leatherback turtles are the largest—they can be more than six feet long and weigh as much as 1,500 pounds!

Leatherback turtle

Sea turtles spend most of their life in the water, eating algae, sea grass, shrimp, crabs, and jellyfish. But once a year, thousands of them come to the beaches and islands of the Great Barrier Reef to lay their eggs.

With its front flippers, the female turtle pulls itself slowly up a sandy beach. It is looking for the perfect spot to make a nest. The sand can't be too powdery or dry. The sea turtle digs out a nest with its back flippers. For the next twenty minutes, it will lay around 120 eggs. Finally, it covers them up with sand and returns to the water.

The temperature inside the nest determines whether the turtles will be born male or female—cooler nests mean males, and warmer ones mean

females. The eggs take two or three months to hatch. After a couple of days of digging, the baby sea turtles all emerge and head straight for the ocean.

The water may be close by, but the trip is dangerous for the two-inch-long babies. Birds and crabs love to eat the hatchlings.

If the turtles make it to the water, they'll take cover in floating seaweed and ride the ocean currents for hundreds, even *thousands* of miles as they feed and grow.

Out in the open ocean, young sea turtles are in constant danger. They can be eaten, or even caught up in fishing nets. They die from eating floating trash, like plastic, which they can mistake for food.

After five or ten years, when the turtles have grown to about the size of a dinner plate, they return to coastal areas to feed, and grow some more. Finally, twenty or more years after hatching, the baby sea turtles are all grown up. Only one out of every thousand hatchlings will make it this far. But when they do, the turtles return to the same area, sometimes the very same beaches, where they hatched.

Baby sea turtles

Yellow-spotted
monitor lizard

Lizard Island, in the northern Great Barrier Reef, is home to—you guessed it—lizards! Captain Cook named the island for its many yellow-spotted monitor lizards. These four-foot-long lizards use their forked tongues to sniff out prey. They can also balance on their back legs and tail to reach their food—like a tasty, crunchy grasshopper high up in a bush!

The largest reptile in the world can also be found on the Great Barrier Reef. The saltwater crocodile—known in Australia as the "saltie"—can grow to more than twenty feet long and weigh more than two thousand pounds! Salties are extremely dangerous. They have been known to attack and kill humans. It's rare, however, to see them swimming among the coral reefs. They prefer swamps, creeks, and lagoons near the shore.

From tiny zooplankton and colorful reef fish, to sharks, crocodiles, and whales, so many creatures live in the Great Barrier Reef. But there is more to their beautiful home than just its coral reefs.

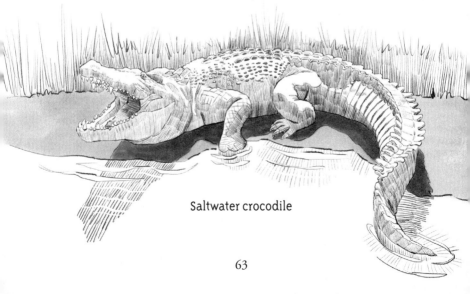

Saltwater crocodile

CHAPTER 5
Rain Forests and Sea Grasslands

A habitat means the place where certain plants and animals naturally live. A rain forest is a type of habitat. So is a coral reef. However, only a very small part (7 percent) of the Great Barrier Reef is made up of actual coral reefs. There are other habitats, too.

A vast lagoon nearly half the size of Texas lies between the Australian coast and the outer reefs. (The outer reefs are those closest to the open ocean.) The lagoon is like a saltwater lake.

Reef

Mainland

Lagoon

Thousands of years ago, before the sea levels rose, this lagoon was dry land, where Aborigines lived. Herds of kangaroos once roamed what is now a sandy underwater habitat. The lagoon can be very shallow, but in some places, it is three hundred feet deep.

The lagoon might look empty, but there is plenty of life in this habitat. Shrimp and goby fish burrow in the sand together. Sea snakes, crabs, starfish, sea cucumbers, worms, and urchins also call the lagoon home.

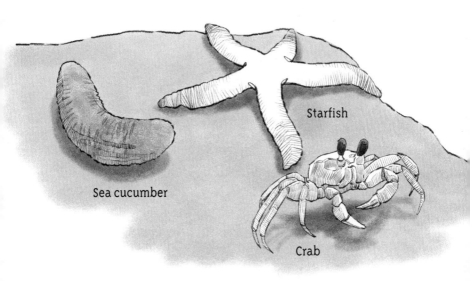

Starfish

Sea cucumber

Crab

Rays glide along the seafloor to search for food hiding in the sand. Great hammerhead sharks patrol the area, too, hunting the rays, their favorite food.

Steve Irwin (1962–2006)

Known as "The Crocodile Hunter," Australian Steve Irwin was one of the world's most famous naturalists. He grew up living and working at his family's zoo and dedicated his life to protecting wildlife. The "saltie" was one of Steve's favorite animals. He would sometimes call the crocodiles "little beauties"—even the big ones.

One day in 2006, Steve and his cameraman were filming an eight-foot-wide stingray in the shallow waters of the Great Barrier Reef lagoon. Suddenly, the stingray began stabbing Steve with its poison stinger. Steve Irwin died soon after.

Patches of feathery soft corals and seaweeds grow in the lagoon. The soft corals serve as nurseries, protecting tiny young fish from predators. As the fish grow up, they move across the floor of the lagoon. They swim from one area of soft coral to another. Then finally they reach the coral reef as adults. Nearly half the fish that live on the coral reef grow up in the lagoon.

In the shallow waters close to shore are underwater meadows of green sea grass. These plants cover about 2,200 square miles of the Great Barrier Reef. That's almost enough sea grass to cover the state of Delaware!

Sea grass is the dugong's favorite food. The dugong (DOO-gong) is a mammal also known as a sea cow. Dugongs can grow to be more than ten feet long. Some weigh close to one thousand pounds. Traveling in groups of up to two hundred, each adult dugong eats its way through eighty pounds of sea grass a day!

Like sea turtles, dugongs were a favorite food of the Aborigines.

Dugongs

Sirenians

Dugongs and manatees belong to a group of animals known as the *sirenians* (sigh-REE-NEE-en). According to legend, they were mistaken for mermaids, or *sirens*.

Elephants are the sirenians' closest living land relatives. Around fifty-five million years ago, sirenians' tails evolved into a large paddle. Their forelegs became shorter. Their back legs and outer fingers disappeared. They developed paddles instead of hands, perfect for steering through the water. But a sirenian's skeleton shows that they still have finger bones.

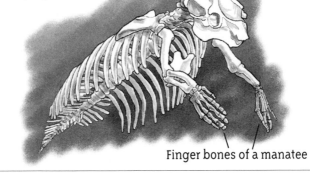

Finger bones of a manatee

Sea-grass beds are more than salad bars for dugongs and sea turtles. Fish live there, too, picking off the bits of algae that grow on the grass. And like the soft-coral patches in the lagoon, the sea-grass beds serve as a nursery for baby fish.

Sea-grass beds also capture sediment. Sediment is a substance that sinks in water. It can be made of soil, sand, twigs, and leaves. Sediment gets from land to sea by rivers and rainwater. Without sea-grass beds to stop it, this sediment would be carried out to the reefs. Why is this important? Sediment would make the water cloudy, and choke the coral.

Mangrove forests are another very important habitat in the Great Barrier Reef. Mangroves are a special kind of tree. They can live in both freshwater and salt water. Much of their roots are actually aboveground, in the open air.

Twice a day, ocean tides flood the mangrove forests with salt water. The salt water mixes with freshwater from rivers that flow into the lagoon. The mangroves' exposed roots slow the flow of water from the freshwater streams. The sediment in the streams then falls to the bottom and won't flow out into the ocean.

This sediment is thick, and rich in organic material. One teaspoon of mangrove mud can contain ten *billion* bacteria. This microscopic super food helps keep the mangroves healthy. It also feeds animals like fiddler crabs and tiny shrimp.

Fiddler crab

Like sea-grass beds, mangroves also serve as a nursery for baby reef fish. The trees' roots provide perfect hiding places from the birds and young reef sharks that hunt in the area.

So where do these streams and rivers full of rich sediment come from? They get their start in the rain forests on the east Australian coast.

These tropical rain forests are the oldest in the world and among the world's wettest places.

It rains there about 120 days a year—with as much as two feet falling in a day! This rain nourishes life in the rain forest. And it feeds the rivers that flow to the mangroves and out into the lagoon.

The different reef habitats depend on one another the same way animals on the Reef do. Rain forest streams provide nutritious sediment for mangrove forests to grow. The healthier the mangroves are, the more sediment they can keep from going out to sea. Whatever the mangroves don't catch, the sea-grass meadows will.

Without these habitats, there would be no safe place for reef fish to grow up. And without the millions of algae-eating fish to keep them clean, the corals of the Great Barrier Reef would be choked to death by green algae.

The outer reef helps protect all these habitats from storms. When hurricanes strike, they hit the outer reef hardest. After winds and waves crash against the reef, the hurricanes become weaker.

Without the outer reefs, these storms would do much greater damage to the shore.

The relationships among the habitats of the Great Barrier Reef are important. But they are also fragile. Overfishing, changes in weather, farming, and pollution all affect the health of the Great Barrier Reef.

Sadly, no period has brought more danger to the Great Barrier Reef than the past 150 years. Until very recently, Australia was still an unexplored continent almost no one knew existed.

Now that has changed.

CHAPTER 6
The Unknown South Land

The Unknown South Land—*Terra Australis Incognita*—existed in people's minds long before European explorers sailed the South Seas.

In 350 BC, the Greek philosopher Aristotle described how the winds from the north—from the Arctic—brought snow and water to the European continent. He imagined there must also be a *southern* continent, where winds blew from the south. This was long before anyone knew the continents of Australia or Antarctica existed.

Aristotle

In the fifth century, a Roman mapmaker called this imaginary southern continent *Australis*. In Latin, that means "south" or "southern."

Some researchers believe that Portuguese sailors spotted the Australian coast from their ships in the early 1500s. But at the time, the rest of this part of the world had been claimed by Spain. The Portuguese kept the discovery a secret.

In 1606, a Dutch explorer named Willem Janszoon landed on the north coast of Australia. He was the first European to set foot on the continent. For the next forty years, Dutch sailors explored the northern and western coasts of the continent. They called it New Holland. As they explored, they drew maps of the areas. Some maps showed the coast connected to Papua New Guinea. But others did not. No one knew yet if Australia was an island.

In the 1760s, an Englishman named Alexander Dalrymple found an old map from 1606. After studying it, Dalrymple believed that *Terra Australis* must be *huge*! He published his ideas, saying the southern continent could be larger than Asia! Dalrymple's work caught the attention of the British government. In 1768, Captain Cook was sent on his famous voyage.

Cook was the first European to explore the east coast of Australia, which he named New

South Wales. He sailed along the coast through the Great Barrier Reef. After exiting the Reef, he headed west through the Torres Strait. Now he saw that *Terra Australis* was separate from Papua New Guinea.

Still, no one knew that Australia was an island until 1803, when Englishman Matthew Flinders sailed all the way around it.

Matthew Flinders

In 1814, Flinders published a book about his journey. He called the southern continent "Australia," saying that it was "more agreeable to the ear" than *Terra Australis*.

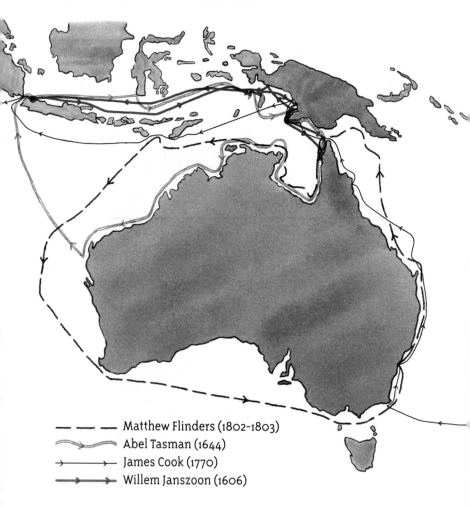

‑ ‑ ‑ ‑ ‑ Matthew Flinders (1802-1803)
Abel Tasman (1644)
James Cook (1770)
Willem Janszoon (1606)

Flinders also named the collection of reefs along Australia's east coast. He called them "the Great Barrier Reefs."

People from England began moving to Australia in 1788, not many years before Flinders's voyage. The first settlement was Sydney, about eight hundred miles south of the Great Barrier Reef. In the 1850s, gold was discovered. More people moved to the continent. As the years went on, people moved farther and farther north—and closer and closer to the Reef.

Australia's First European Settlers

The first English settlers in Australia did not come by choice. They were prisoners.

Eighteenth-century England was changing fast. The population was growing, and people began moving from the country to the cities in huge numbers. At the same time, machinery began to do the jobs people used to do. Many people lost work and became poor. Crimes like stealing rose quickly, and prisons became overcrowded. So the government began sending convicts overseas to work off their sentences.

For a long time, England sent prisoners to America. But after the United States declared its independence in 1776, this had to stop. Australia was the natural next choice.

So in 1787, a fleet of eleven ships sailed from England to Australia. The ships were carrying supplies, marine officers, and almost eight hundred convicts. The journey took eight months. In January 1788, they settled in Port Jackson. The captain of the fleet called it "the finest harbor in the world." He named their new settlement Sydney.

By 1840, 150,000 convicts had been shipped to Australia. But now free men and women in England were also choosing to make a new home on the distant continent. The last convict ship landed in Australia in 1868. By 2015, Australia was home to more than twenty-three million people.

The Barrier Reef was rich in natural resources that could be shipped all over the world. By 1860, three major seaports were built along the Reef's coastline.

Islands in the lagoon became coconut plantations and limestone quarries. Trees were chopped down for firewood. Sea turtles, dugongs, and birds were hunted—for food and for sport. Oyster beds disappeared. Reef fish and sea cucumbers were hauled out of the sea by the ton.

On the mainland, forests were cleared to make way for farms and cattle ranches. Swamps were drained to plant sugarcane. Runoff and sediment

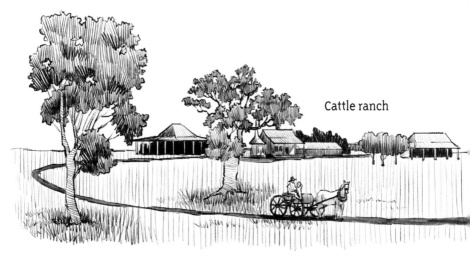

Cattle ranch

poured into the lagoon. Harmful chemicals followed, once the use of fertilizers became more widespread. Coral along the shoreline and sea-grass meadows began to die out.

The habitats of the Great Barrier Reef were suffering.

Also suffering were the native peoples. The Aboriginal and Torres Strait Islander tribes of the Reef had lived on this land for thousands of years. Now it was being taken away from them. The Aborigines fought back for more than a hundred years. But they were no match for the settlers' firepower. By the 1930s, perhaps more than thirty thousand Aborigines—and more than two thousand white Australians—had been killed. Sickness brought over from Europe killed even more Aborigines than the settlers' guns. By the time Australia became an independent country, as many as nine out of every ten native Australians had died from disease or violence.

Even after the fighting ended, native Australians were treated as second-class citizens for many years. The Australian government took Aboriginal children away from their parents to train them as servants. Aborigines were made to assimilate, or

become more like white Australians. They were removed from their homelands and sent to cities.

Until the 1960s, Aborigines were segregated, or separated, from white Australians in places like movie theaters and hospitals. In some areas, they were not allowed to vote until 1962.

From the 1960s until today, the Australian government has been gradually trying to fix the wrongs of the past. Since 1971, more than thirty Aborigines—many of them women—have been elected to Australia's state, territorial, and federal governments. Today, Aborigines make up about 3 percent of the country's population, and they have many more rights than they once did. But they still face prejudice and racism.

Neville Bonner,
Australia's first Aboriginal
member of Parliament

Ghost Ships

During the 1800s, early maps of the Great Barrier Reef were incomplete. Traveling through it was dangerous. Since coral grows taller every year, the safe pathways were always changing. Because of this, there were many shipwrecks.

When some Reef tribes first met shipwrecked Europeans, they thought the pale-faced sailors must be ghosts—ghosts of dead relatives who had now come back on ghost ships.

As for the Europeans, they told tall tales about these Reef natives. Some described them as cruel and murderous "savages." But almost always, the natives helped any castaways they met.

CHAPTER 7
"Save the Reef!"

Two books published in 1893 and 1908 brought the natural wonders of the Great Barrier Reef to the world's attention.

William Saville-Kent studied the Reef for four years. He discovered many species of fish and coral. He created detailed color sketches of as much as he could. He even photographed fish in a portable "aquarium" made out of a giant clamshell.

His book, *The Great Barrier Reef of Australia*, was published in 1893 and became a total sensation. People around the world now knew about the Great Barrier Reef.

In 1896, Ted Banfield and his wife, Bertha, visited Dunk Island in the Great Barrier Reef lagoon. They fell in love with the place. The very next year—with help from local islanders—they built a cabin. The Banfields ended up staying for years. *The Confessions of a Beachcomber*—Ted's 1908 book about their life on the island—also became a worldwide best seller.

The Banfields

Suddenly, everyone wanted to see what the Great Barrier Reef was all about!

In the 1920s, resorts began to pop up on islands in the lagoon. Visitors swam among the coral reefs. They went spearfishing. They watched sea turtles lay their eggs.

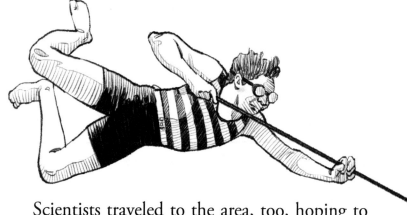

Scientists traveled to the area, too, hoping to learn more about the Reef.

In 1922, a group of scientists warned that the resorts were damaging the Reef. But tourists continued to visit well into the 1960s.

The Reef became polluted with sewage and trash. Tourists snatched bits of coral and shells as

souvenirs. Reefs were blown up, and forests were cleared to make room for airstrips, marinas, and passageways for boats. Entire sections of the Great Barrier Reef began to die. Fishermen noticed their catches were smaller, and the water was getting cloudier. When the government began selling sections of the Reef to oil companies, things had gone far enough. Now it was time for people to take action.

In 1967, a poet, an artist, and a scientist came together to create "Save the Reef." The campaign leaders—Judith Wright, John Busst, and Len Webb—wanted to raise awareness of what was happening. They wanted to stop companies from drilling for oil there. They hoped to make Australians feel like the Great Barrier Reef belonged to all of them—and that they were responsible for its well-being.

Judith Wright

John Busst

Len Webb

The governor of the state of Queensland called them "nitwits" and "rat-bags." He hired his own scientist to do a study. The scientist said that the

Reef *should* be drilled for oil. He also suggested that coral be mined for its limestone. It could be ground up to make fertilizer and cement!

Then, in 1969, a disaster occurred far away. An oil rig off the California coast sprung a huge leak. Video footage of dead fish, oil-covered seabirds, and black beaches flashed across Australian TV screens. The governor still insisted that this would *never* happen in the Great Barrier Reef. Another government official suggested that since the oil was protein, it would be nutritious for the fish and other marine life.

Australians did not believe them!

Finally, the government listened to the concerned Australian citizens. In 1975, the Great Barrier Reef Marine Park Act became law. It

Australian Government

Great Barrier Reef Marine Park Authority

protected the Reef from mining and drilling. "Save the Reef" had won!

A national park was established. Along with it, many rules were made for visiting the park. For example, there were limits to how close boats could get to a whale or dolphin. The new law also divided the Reef into different zones. In some zones, fishing and shipping were allowed, but in others, they were not. The law aimed to protect the Reef for generations to come.

Aborigines and Torres Strait Islanders are allowed to continue their hunting traditions to this day. However, the number of sea turtles and dugongs they can kill is limited.

In 1981, the Great Barrier Reef was named a

World Heritage Site by the United Nations. This protected it even more from drilling and harmful human activities. Only places "of outstanding universal value" to humankind are given this honor. For example, the Great Wall of China and the Grand Canyon are also World Heritage Sites.

However, the Great Barrier Reef still faces many dangers. Coal plants are being built on the mainland. To send this coal to other parts of the world, Australian seaports are being made bigger. This involves dredging, or digging out sand and soil from the seabed. All the digging means more sediment gets dumped into the Great Barrier Reef.

A dredger

More ships traveling through the Reef has resulted in more accidents. In 2010, a cargo ship full of coal crashed into a coral reef at full speed. It left a scar along the reef nearly two miles long. The boat almost fell apart. Four tons of fuel leaked into the water.

Perhaps the greatest danger the Reef faces is climate change.

Around the world, temperatures are rising. Most coral cannot survive for long in water that is warmer than eighty-eight degrees Fahrenheit. Above this temperature, the algae inside the polyps produce too much oxygen. When this happens, the polyps expel the algae, driving out their little food-factories.

Algae are what give the coral its color. Once the coral pushes the algae out, the coral turns ghostly white. This process is called coral bleaching. Coral can survive for a few weeks after bleaching. But without the algae to produce its food, it will die.

The years 2014 and 2015 were the hottest on record. By early 2016, coral bleaching was occurring across the globe. The Great Barrier Reef suffered the most. Scientists looked at more than five hundred reefs in the Reef's northern areas. They found *just four reefs* without any bleaching.

Another danger the Reef faces is from chemical changes in ocean water. As the world continues to burn fossil fuels like coal and oil, more and more carbon dioxide (CO_2) is pumped into the air. Much of this CO_2 is absorbed by the oceans, turning the water *acidic*. Acidic water breaks down corals. And too

Coal plant

much CO_2 in the water means the corals can't grow their carbon skeletons and enlarge the reef. Scientists worry that as early as 2050, coral reefs around the world might start to dissolve.

As world temperatures rise, hurricanes are becoming stronger and more numerous. These hurricanes bring strong winds and powerful waves that break apart reefs, killing the coral. Two powerful hurricanes struck Queensland and the Great Barrier Reef in 2011 and 2014. With wind gusts of over 150 miles per hour, they were the strongest hurricanes to hit the area in almost one hundred years. More are sure to come.

Warmer temperatures are also melting the world's glaciers and ice caps. Sea levels are rising. Sea-turtle eggs on the Great Barrier Reef's tiny islands are in danger of being drowned.

In the last thirty years, *half* the coral on the Great Barrier Reef has died. The fight that began in the 1960s to "Save the Reef" is far from over.

To preserve this magnificent and beautiful natural wonder, everyone must do their part. As the poet Judith Wright once said of the Great Barrier Reef: "We have its fate in our hands."

Timeline of the Great Barrier Reef and Australia

c. 100,000 BC	Earth becomes colder; sea levels begin to drop
c. 50,000 BC	Aborigines arrive in Australia
c. 16,000–4000 BC	Earth warms; sea levels rise; lagoon and islands form
c. 10,000 BC	Aborigines begin to tell the story of the Great Flood
c. 7000 BC	Great Barrier Reef begins to grow
AD 1522	Portuguese sailors are the first Europeans to spot Australia
1606	Dutch explorers are the first Europeans to land in Australia
1770	Captain Cook discovers the Great Barrier Reef, names east Australia "New South Wales" and claims it for England
1788	First ship of English convicts arrives in New South Wales
1803	Matthew Flinders sails around Australia, proves it's an island
1814	Flinders names Australia and the Great Barrier Reef
1824	First colony for prisoners in Queensland is established
1868	Last ship of English convicts arrives in Australia
1893	*The Great Barrier Reef of Australia* is published
1901	Australia becomes an independent nation on January 1
1908	*The Confessions of a Beachcomber* is published
1920s	Tourist resorts begin to pop up around the Reef
1967	"Save the Reef" campaign started
1975	The Great Barrier Reef Marine Park Act becomes law
1981	Great Barrier Reef named a UNESCO World Heritage Site
2016	Coral bleaching affects more than 90 percent of the Reef

Timeline of the World

c. 200,000 BC	*Homo sapiens*—modern humans—begin to evolve
c. 40,000 BC	Neanderthals become extinct
c. 2540 BC	Great Pyramid of Khufu is completed in Egypt
c. 2000 BC	Woolly mammoth becomes extinct
c. AD 1503	Leonardo da Vinci paints the *Mona Lisa*
1605	Cervantes's *Don Quixote de la Mancha* is published
1770	American colonists and British soldiers clash in the Boston Massacre
1789	US Constitution is signed
1803	Thomas Jefferson signs the Louisiana Purchase with France, doubling the size of the United States
1826	World's first photograph is taken
1858	First can opener is patented in the United States
1893	New Zealand gives women the right to vote
1901	Vacuum cleaner is invented
1909	National Association for the Advancement of Colored People (NAACP) is founded
1969	Woodstock music festival held in Bethel, New York
1974	US president Richard Nixon resigns
1981	Sandra Day O'Connor becomes the first female US Supreme Court Justice
2012	Superstorm Sandy strikes the northeast United States

Bibliography

Associated Press in Brisbane. "Chinese Ship Runs Aground on Great Barrier Reef." *The Guardian*, April 4, 2010. http://www.theguardian.com/world/2010/apr/04/great-barrier-reef-ship-aground.

"Coral Seas." *Blue Planet*. Directed by Alastair Fothergill. BBC/Discovery Channel, 2011.

The Great Barrier Reef. Directed by Richard Fitzpatrick. BBC/Digital Dimensions/Discovery Channel, in association with the Nine Network Australia, 2012.

Innis, Michelle. "Climate-Related Death of Coral Around the World Alarms Scientists." *The New York Times*. April 9, 2016. http://www.nytimes.com/2016/04/10/world/asia/climate-related-death-of-coral-around-world-alarms-scientists.html.

McCalman, Iain. *The Reef: A Passionate History: The Great Barrier Reef from Captain Cook to Climate Change*. New York: Scientific American/Farrar, Straus and Giroux, 2013.

Zell, Len. *The Great Barrier Reef: A Journey Through the World's Greatest Natural Wonder*. Millers Point, New South Wales, and London: Murdoch Books, 2012.

Websites

www.gbrmpa.gov.au (Great Barrier Reef Marine Park Authority)
www.coral.org (Coral Reef Alliance)